Themed Meditations
...along the quiet path

SIMON COLE

Copyright © 2015 Simon Cole

All rights reserved.

ISBN: 979-10-93362-07-6

DEDICATION

To the many who have accompanied a part of the journey

CONTENTS

Introduction   5

The Meditations

1. ...on being alive   12
2. ...watching and waiting   14
3. ...on being just who I am   18
4. ...touching gently   20
5. ...being the flow   24
6. ...to feel at ease   28
7. ...today, tomorrow   30
8. ...feeling inner strength   34
9. ...yin, yang   39
10. ...inside, outside   45
11. ...letting in the world   49
12. ...to release the tension   52
13. ...letting be   56
14. ...to walk in harmony   58
15. ...on the experience of peace   61
16. ...of benevolence for our world   64

About the Author   67

ACKNOWLEDGEMENTS

How can we know the role of others? No way to know, only wonder, and accept that I wouldn't be here if they hadn't been there; clients, students, voices, companions, fellow travellers, and of course family, all of them part of the story

Introduction

Themed Meditations ...along the quiet path

Themed meditations are different from guided visualisations and other more image-based forms of prompted meditation.

As a non-directive counsellor, I believe that we are the only ones who can truly understand ourselves; and because that understanding forms the basis of our way of being in the world - how we act, how we relate, how we move forward with our lives - it is important that it is not distorted by any external frame of reference. Meditation is one of the ways in which our self-understanding can be developed and enhanced and so, from my counsellor's perspective, it is important that as little as possible is 'planted' into the process.

When I formalised the Clear Space Meditation Path (set out in "Stillness in Mind"), after years of using mindfulness and meditation alongside the therapeutic process with clients, I held to this principle. But I also recognised how people's needs in coming to a meditation practice varied. And so I introduced themed meditations as a way to provide a framework for their practice which still left their process unhindered and lucid. However, I do not want to suggest that anyone would need or want to use such themes all the time, though equally I think that there will be some occasions on which anyone might find a theme of benefit. And so, I suggest that you use them according to your own pattern and preference.

Each meditation has an introductory text and then the narration of the meditation itself. The introduction is intended for contemplation and to 'set the scene'. You may find you simply want to use it to lend an atmosphere to your sitting, or you may want to spend longer with it, ponder it and let your own ideas develop from it. Then when you are ready, move on to the narration of the meditation.

Breathing

In the narrations, I refer to "long breaths". It is important to understand this as referring to long (and slow) breathing and not deep breathing of the sort we use to catch our breath. The latter is invariably chest breathing, but I am meaning the sort of breathing a singer or a wind-player uses. To do this, relax your chest muscles and, without forcing anything, keep your shoulders and chest from rising as you breathe. Now draw the breath right down through your diaphragm, possibly letting your stomach swell as you reach the end of each breath. Breathe steadily and slowly. Ensure that you breathe out at the same rate and to the same extent. Breathing in this way, in beginning your meditation, will help you to relax your muscles and to create the clear space and stillness that helps your sitting.

Think-relax

Sometimes I use the expression "think-relax". This refers to using our mind to bring about muscle-relaxation without any physical routine. It needs practice on its own. A picture can help. Imagine a tuned guitar with its strings taut and notice what that looks like. This is your muscles when they are tense. Now imagine the same guitar as if all the pegs which hold the strings had been loosened - the strings are limp and wavy. This is your muscles when they are relaxed. Look from the first picture to the second in your mind and, as you do this, let your muscles reflect the changing image. Practise this with the images in your mind and then start to do it without. You are training your mind to respond directly to the thought and it will enable you to "think-relax": because it is your mind which is controlling your muscles when they are tense, so it is your mind which will release them.

Mantra words

Because these are themed meditations and not guided visualisations, it is not essential to remember the exact text. The words and phrases are carefully chosen, but it is more important that you allow them to create an atmosphere and a soft framework for your sitting. But to help you retain the theme to the extent you want to, you will find in the narration sections a small number of words or short phrases highlighted in bold and non-italicized. After reading the narration a couple of times you can go to these 'mantra words' to hold in your mind during your sitting in order to stay closer to the narration. Some of them you might find lend themselves to spoken repetition during your sitting. But however you use them, the most important consideration is that it fits with what is most comfortable and helpful for you.

Themed Meditations ...along the quiet path

Simon Cole

The Meditations

1 ...*on being alive*

Complete stillness is an illusion. All around us there is movement... sap rising, hearts beating, water flowing, wind blowing...

Every sound we hear has living connected to it... birds which are singing, neighbours who are talking, a car being driven, a plane carrying people...

Yes, complete stillness, is an illusion.

There are probably 8.7 million species (remaining) on earth, of which we have catalogued around 1.2 million, of which Man is only one. There is that much living going on. That much turning, beating, oozing, swirling, gliding, floating, swinging, wriggling, curling, rising, falling, sliding, hatching, swaying, galloping, waving, going on... of which we do a tiny fraction.

This meditation is about feeling our place and connecting to that life energy and allowing the movement of all that living to rise in us and draw us in.

Start with three long breaths and allow your out-breaths to smoothe the tensions in your muscles so that you can feel your whole body ease and relax...

Let your breathing subside into a gentle even rhythm...

Feel yourself moving into your clear space...

With your eyes closed, start to notice the sounds around you, the sounds of the outside world coming to you...

Behind every sound there is something living, so go to each in turn as you notice it and simply be with the sound, without even telling yourself that you like it or that you don't like it, only that there is living there...

Stay close to it for a few moments, not describing its origin, not visualising, but sensing the life that is connected to it...

Now go to another sound, and another...

*Sense yourself **amongst all this living** that you have been touching, alongside it, a part of it, not the centre...*

Feel your one-ness with this movement and this life around you and feel it rise in you like a wind surging and uplifting you...

When you are ready, after your usual time of sitting, lengthen your breathing into three long breaths to bring yourself back.

2 ...*watching and waiting*

Watching and waiting sometimes seems to be all we can do and sometimes seems to be what we are doing for long periods of our lives. Time passes and our lives go by and we cease to be shapers of our own destiny.

But if we could watch without waiting...

Watching can only be watching of what is here and now. Waiting takes us beyond the edge of now.

Beyond now is nowhere. But we must live somewhere; a somewhere which can only be here and now... and not waiting.

Prepare yourself by sitting comfortably: check and physically loosen the muscles which you find are most apt to tense up for you...

Take three long breaths, as slowly and steadily as is comfortable...

... think-relax ...

Allow your breathing to subside to a normal rate, as if coming down a gentle slope, and notice the slope becoming level ground and your breathing steady and smooth and even...

Notice the smoothness and evenness of your breathing...

Feel the ease of your clear space...

Turn your attention to one of your senses, perhaps your hearing, and focus on one of the sounds which is coming to you...

For a few moments let this sound be all that your sense of hearing is bringing to you...

Now return to your breathing and your clear space...

When you are ready, go to another of your senses in the same way, perhaps touch, and for a few moments focus on one place you can **feel the contact** *of something, perhaps a coolness in the air, perhaps the cushion beneath you, perhaps one hand touching the other...*

For a few moments let this touch be all that is coming to you...

Now return to your breathing and your clear space...

Go in turn to each of your other senses - smell, taste and sight and each time do the same...

Each time return to your breathing and your clear space, letting go of the sense which you have been holding...

Let your sitting consist of this cycle of joining with each of your senses, allowing what comes from each to be what you hold for those few moments...

When you are ready to return, gradually lengthen your breathing, finally taking three long breaths to bring you back.

Themed Meditations ...along the quiet path

3 ...on being just who I am

We have lived these many years and we must value all that they have brought.

We have trodden so many roads and still could feel the buzz of starting here.

We have met so many others who have shaped the one we are and all should have a place because of who we are, and because we must respect the one we are, prizing our story for all its many parts.

We cannot love others unless we love ourselves and we cannot love ourselves unless we love this person here and now... with all their many parts, and for everything they are.

Here is a meditation to help to integrate a true sense of the person you are.

Start with three long breaths and allow your out-breaths to smoothe the tensions in your muscles so that you can feel your whole body ease and relax...

Let your breathing subside into a gentle even rhythm as you move into your clear space...

When you are at ease in your clear space, turn your attention onto yourself, but don't look inward, rather feel your whole self, sitting as your are...

Allow a sense to develop of being both the observer and the observed, seeing and being seen almost in the same instant...

Notice without judgment the different parts of you, both what is visible on the outside and what only you know on the inside, and treat everything that comes into your mind equally, nothing is good and nothing is bad, but here **everything is simply a part**...

As you notice more and more parts of you, aspects of your life, people you know past and present, each with a place in your story, be aware of the sense of you and these parts and let them all form into a thread which comes through your life to this moment now...

Let your sense of the thread, your life, you as the observer and the observed, and where you are now, all merge into one...

Look for a feeling of ease within yourself and turn your focus to it...

When you are ready, after your usual time of sitting, lengthen your breathing into three long breaths to bring yourself back.

4 ...*touching gently*

On a hot day the line of the horizon shimmers in the heat haze; in the cool dusk of the evening the sea shades perfectly into the greying sky; in a gentle breeze the leaf-mantle of the solid elm blurs against its backdrop. I trail my hand through the long grass and feel its breathless touch brush my fingers.

Sometimes it can be good to allow life's harsh outlines to blur a little. These days we circumscribe our lives with exactness - times, regulations, schedules, procedures - "to make it easier", we tell ourselves, "so that we know where we are". But the frame in which we find ourselves - mostly of our own making - and which seems to give shape to our lives, can also mean we never look at how things *might* be... the other side of the line of action we have self-prescribed.

This meditation is about softening that edge, looking beyond the line, touching gently.

Sit comfortably in your chosen space, with your back erect and holding your head so that you are looking straight out ahead of you, whether you are looking out at a view or at the interior of the room...

Notice what you are looking at so that, if someone asked, you could describe what you are seeing, but then gradually release your thoughts from what your eyes are seeing, so that what is in front of you is no more than a collection of shapes on which light is shining...

Bring your attention to your breathing and let it be as smooth and even as you are able...

As you follow your breath, notice the 'in' and 'out' of your breathing, the lifting and falling, the pausing and releasing...

Stay with these sensations in the front of your mind for a few moments and then let them gradually drift to the back until they are no more than what is going on...

As the sensations of your breathing drift to the back of your mind, turn your awareness to the sensation of sitting, the immediate physical sensation of being supported at the base of your spine with your back erect, resting on your seat...

After a few moments allow the sensations of your sitting to become dull as they drift back in your mind...

Now bring into your mind with as much clarity and vividness as you can an image which represents the life you are living now...

After a few moments while you are still looking at this image take your mind back to the sensation of your breathing, noticing the 'in' and 'out', the **lifting and falling**, *the* **pausing and releasing**...

Repeat the cycle of awareness through breathing, sitting and seeing as many times as you wish...

When you are ready to end your sitting, gradually lengthen your breathing, finally taking three long breaths to bring you back.

Themed Meditations ...along the quiet path

5 ...*being the flow*

Because we look at things around us and register what they are, or what they mean, or how they are affecting us, in order to know how to react, we mostly process life in slices. You could say that each thing we look at we 'fix' while we work it out.

But change, which is happening all around all the time, isn't a series of slices. So living can't be either.

We have a problem. The brain needs time - yes, nanoseconds, I know - to tell us the size and shape of things, but our living is going on all the time. So we no sooner get a handle on something than we're past it! We are always slightly out of sync with the world around us.

This meditation is for when it would be good to be with the flow, without working anything out, just open to what is around. It is to help achieve a sense of being at one with what is around us by moving in step with all we are sensing. It is better to use this idea of sensing rather than looking in a visual way, thereby not making anything an object but rather feeling it as something living, which is changing alongside us as we change.

Prepare yourself by sitting comfortably: check and physically loosen the muscles which you find are most apt to tense up for you...

... think-relax ...

Take three long breaths, as slowly and steadily as is comfortable...

... think-relax ...

Let your breathing gradually subside into a normal and easy rhythm...

In the few moments before thought intrudes, notice your body from the inside and any 'floatiness' or 'fuzziness', wherever you find it...

As any thoughts appear, notice them as your thinking; perhaps you can say to yourself that it is your thinking and then be able to feel a release from the thought as you return to your breathing..

Bring into your mind a sense of yourself as you are sitting and then a sense of your **world** *in all its many aspects* **alongside and around** *you...*

Move between these two senses and each time notice a new aspect of your world as it comes to you, in whatever way it comes, whether sound or image or feel. Take time to really notice each one before you return to your sense of yourself. Then move to another aspect of your world..

Now let go of you and your world being separate entities, and allow you with your world to exist **as a unity**...

Notice how the aspects which you sensed before are alongside and part of this one existence and moving with you and you with them...

Feel the flow of this existence, giving your attention to the different aspects as pure awareness, without describing or explaining or interpreting..

When you are ready to close, hold your awareness of your own body for a few moments, before lengthening your breathing as you come out of your meditation.

Themed Meditations ...along the quiet path

6 ...to feel at ease

To be anxious is to be human. Very few people can say that there is nothing that makes them anxious. And so there are very few people who don't at some time know what it's like to feel that unease which can for some quicken the breathing and lead to a dizzying sense of foreboding and claustrophobic vulnerability.

In some cases anxiety seems specific. In others it is more like a general feeling of unsafeness about the world and living. But one thing all anxiety has in common is that its object, its real object, is not here and now, even though its source, which lies within us, is.

This is a meditation to bring an easing of the upsetting discomfort which accompanies anxiety; and points a way to being able to cope more easily when the feeling begins.

Prepare yourself by sitting comfortably: check and physically loosen the muscles which you find are most apt to tense up for you...

... think-relax ...

Take three long breaths, as slowly and steadily as is comfortable...

... think-relax ...

As your breathing subsides, start to 'stroke' yourself with your out-breath, noticing how you can give it more force if your mind leans the weight of your body into it... and now you can have a sense of your breath just floating in to your body when you breathe in and gently stroking you as you breathe out...

Hold this pattern for several minutes, if possible with nothing else going on in your mind, and return to it whenever you come back to your clear space as thoughts disperse...

As you feel your out-breath stroking you, feel your mind being pulled away from thoughts and resting with your body; notice that the only place you need to be is here with this gentle caress. Go back to this at regular intervals as you sit.

In your mind you could play yourself the mantra:

gently being, being now

When you are ready to close, hold your awareness of your own body for a few moments, before lengthening your breathing as you come out of your meditation.

7 ...*today,* **tomorrow**

Life is going to be different tomorrow. A change is coming. The road we are travelling is going to look different, and will be different. That much we know. But what will have changed or how is something else. Perhaps, deep down inside, in our body or in our mind, the answer is already there, but hidden from us. The change has already happened. Or perhaps the change will come from outside... the answer somewhere else, but, today, hidden from us.

This much we know: tomorrow it will have changed, the life we are living.

Themed Meditations ...along the quiet path

Prepare yourself by sitting comfortably: check and physically loosen the muscles which you find are most apt to tense up for you...

Take three long breaths, as slowly and steadily as is comfortable...

In your tension, your mind is outside your body, its thoughts coiling round you like a spring, so bring it back in, joining with your body...

As you let your breathing subside to a normal rhythm, draw your mind in to be a part of your physical being supported by the earth...

*Your physical being is still and sits erect, so your **mind can uncoil** and start to feel its stillness...*

Notice the comfort of your clear space and hold it precious...

Don't try to hold your clear space unmoving, because change is happening all around all the time and living is a flow...

Allow each moment to flow into the next...

Yesterday's moments flowed into today and today contained them...

*Today's moments will flow into tomorrow and **tomorrow will contain** them...*

Your clear space will go with you into tomorrow...

Your mind uncoiled can be with you tomorrow...

Remain now in your clear space with no more than your sense of each moment flowing into the next, today in the process of becoming tomorrow...

When you are ready to return, gradually lengthen your breathing, finally taking three long breaths to end your sitting.

Themed Meditations ...along the quiet path

8 ...feeling inner strength

There are times when we feel that the whole world's against us and when there seems to be no way to get past all the difficulties and obstacles which are in our way. And then it seems as if, whichever way we might turn, there will be something hemming us in, people against us, circumstances against us, our past against us, and that right in this moment we have nothing left in the tank, nothing with which to break out and breathe freely again.

At these times a feeling of helplessness can start to take over. We look at everything that's against us and start to wonder how we could ever find the strength to battle through our difficulties and feel normal again. And then we might find ourselves wondering whether it would not be easier to give up the fight rather than have to face constant failure. And we start to close in on ourselves, because it's easier not to have to face the outside world, easier not to look people in the eye, easier to just accept that nothing is ever going to be any different. We resign ourselves to how things are; and in some ways that feels easier and gives a little relief. Until the world seems to close around us even more and resignation turns to hopelessness with no end even imaginable.

This meditation is for those times when we notice that our energy is short because of all that has been happening to us, and we are at risk of closing in on ourselves and wishing the world away because it is becoming too much to face.

For this sitting it is important to be in a space which is not too small; have clear space all around you and an open space in front of you; if you are inside and it is not unbearable because of cold or noise, have a window open.

Ensure that your position of sitting is such that your spine is naturally erect and your head held so that your eye-line is horizontal.

With this meditation you can loop back to an earlier stage where you begin to feel your strength beginning, making sure each time that you build on where you are.

The theme is one of feeling this growing strength, combined with opening up and looking wide, to counter the closing down and drawing in which at times we all experience.

Prepare yourself by sitting comfortably: check and physically loosen the muscles which you find are most apt to tense up for you...

... think-relax ...

Take three long breaths, as slowly and steadily as is comfortable...

... think-relax ...

Let your breathing gradually subside into a normal and easy rhythm...

When your breathing is steady and smooth, notice how you are being supported by the floor or the ground on which you are sitting; feel your weight as it is passing down through your spine, ultimately into the earth below you...

As you gain a sense of being supported in this way, increase the length of your breaths a little and hold them at this new steady rate to complement the grounded firmness of your body held by the earth...

From your seat feel a sense of solid strength pass slowly up through your spine, while you add force (but not length or speed) to your breathing...

As the swell of strength rises through your spine, allow **a lifting and an opening** *out of your being; as the swell reaches your head, open your eyes and take in the space in which you are sitting, but without needing to look at anything in particular...*

Bring into your mind the space beyond the space you can see and the space beyond that and on and on until your space is the whole world...

Spread your arms and stretch your body as you come out of this meditation.

9 ... *yin yang*

Where is the line between good and bad, between light and dark, between known and not known? There is little that we can do which is good for **us**, but which does not limit what someone **else** can do. From a shady room in which we see clearly, we go out into the bright sun and are blinded, so we cover our eyes and we still see lights. So much of what we **know** originates from what we can **see**, but what we can see is relative to the range of wave-lengths our eyes can receive - if that range were more one way or the other along the electro-magnetic spectrum then things that are seen would disappear and things that exist, but are unseen, would appear.

Where is the line which isn't a line?

The picture of yin and yang does not depict two contrasting 'colours', it defines a relation, the relation we set up as we look at the image. And since we are the sole source of the imaging as we look at it, it is indivisible; rather than parts, it has different aspects which contrast only as a consequence of each other.

We see only what we *can* see; what we *do* see has form only as it is *given* form.

This meditation is to help towards a loosening of the certainties we hold which limit our view of our relationship to others.

Prepare yourself by sitting comfortably: check and physically loosen the muscles which you find are most apt to tense up for you...

Take three long breaths, as slowly and steadily as is comfortable...

As your breathing subsides and you move into your clear space, let your attention alternate between the sounds of the world around you and your physical presence sitting supported by the earth...

Resting in your clear space, bring into your awareness a more vivid sense of your physical being, sitting erect, with your weight from your head through your spine passing down to the earth...

This is your presence to yourself...

Now turn your attention to your world around you, especially the sounds, noticing each in turn and then their whole landscape...

After a few moments turn back to your presence to yourself, and then repeat this moving out and moving in again...

Returning now to your presence to yourself, let your consciousness of yourself being the sitter fade so that what remains is the __sense__ of sitting only, the uprightness of your back, the weight of your body being passed through to the earth...

After a while start to hear again the sounds of your world around you, go to each one and be with it for a few moments, and then the next and the next and then the sense of your sitting too, as part of the cycle...

Keep moving through this cycle of your **world around** *you and your sense of your sitting...*

When you are ready to return, let the space clear and gradually lengthen your breathing, finally taking three long breaths to end your sitting.

Themed Meditations ...along the quiet path

Simon Cole

10 ...inside, outside

In preparation for this meditation take a sheet of plain paper, A3 if possible, set it in landscape in front of you and draw a line with a thick felt pen down the centre but leaving a substantial gap at the top and the bottom.

Now on the left side of the line list three or four aspects of yourself - single words or very short phrases - which only you would be able to name in this way. Against each on the right put down a word to describe how others might experience this part of you. For example you might know yourself as self-conscious, so put this on the left; you might believe that this would mean that others would see you as awkward in company, so put that on the right. Or you might know that your mind zooms from one thing to another, so you could put "zooming" on the left and on the right, perhaps, "impetuous" if that's how you think you come across.

Finally, in the spaces above and below the line, enter two aspects of yourself which you believe look the same on the inside and the outside.

You can make this exercise as simple or elaborate as you like: if you want to do it in colour, that is fine, or you might draw little sketches to represent each of the words, and maybe the sketches will be more informative than the writing. However you do it, spend a few moments before you start your meditation, quietly perusing what you have created.

Prepare yourself by sitting comfortably: check and physically loosen the muscles which you find are most apt to tense up for you...

Take three long breaths then start to let your rate of breathing subside and, as you do this, pause very slightly at the end of each in-breath and each out-breath and notice the sensations of the air contained and the air released...

Return to these, the air contained and the air released, at intervals during this meditation...

Let an aspect of yourself come into your mind and rest your attention on it for a few moments, not needing to be aware of where it was in your landscape, or whether it was there at all, **simply allowing** *it to be what it is...*

As you feel moved, go to another aspect and then another, each time simply noticing, without judging and without telling a story about it...

When you are ready to return, wait for your clear space, gradually lengthening your breathing, finally taking three long breaths to end your sitting.

Simon Cole

11 ...letting in the world

One of the ways in which we block ourselves just when we're in need of some relief from our stress, or from getting ourselves wound up about something that isn't working, or maybe from simply having a down on ourselves because we don't seem to get anything right and we feel a failure; one of the ways in which we block ourselves is to shut ourselves off from the world. We usually don't notice we're doing it. It's not that we're deliberately setting up barriers, but a barrier is there nonetheless. What has happened is that we have turned in on ourselves; our mind has become completely absorbed with what is going on inside. We have been taken over, if you like, by our own introspection and confined in a tunnel, into which nothing from the outside world can penetrate and which is so long that we can't even see the light at the end.

Sometimes we might get a glimpse of what is happening, like when we are angry and we can hear ourselves say inside, "I'm really angry about that and I'm going to stay angry, I'm not going to let it go, I'm not going to budge". At other times it might feel like we are simply trapped, because the tension we feel from everything that is hemming us in is like a wire mesh too tight for us to break through.

It is probably true that at this point it isn't possible to solve everything that is going wrong. It is also true that to try to use meditation to find specific solutions is not a good practise. What these sort of situations call for, and what all meditation has the potential to provide, is a freeing up, a widening of our field of vision, an opening up to the world around us - the aspects of living which stress and distress close off.

This meditation is about reversing that process of closing off. Prepare for it by taking a few moments, after you are sitting comfortably but before you start your initial breathing, to bring into your mind your main concern at the moment, not the whole of it or a lot of detail about it, but simply a headline such as you might see in a newspaper if it were someone else's story. Hold it in your thoughts for a few moments without actually thinking about it. Now bring to mind anything that occurs to you which isn't this, as if you had turned the page in the newspaper and here was a completely different story. Look at this for a few moments and then let both go, as you put the paper down.

Check that you are sitting comfortably: check and physically loosen the muscles which you find are most apt to tense up for you...

Take three long breaths, as slowly and steadily as is comfortable...

Let your breathing subside to a rate which is comfortable for you and when you reach this, notice that it can be an invisible movement on which your attention rests...

Hold your attention more and more on the movement itself and the feelings it creates in your body...

Notice how your body draws in and gives back out and be aware of the turning point as the one becomes the other...

You draw in from around you the air that gives you life and give back out the breath of your being...

The turning point as 'in' becomes 'out' is **like a door swinging one way then the other, marking a passage**, *nowhere being fixed, never still...*

Let your attention settle on the flow of drawing in and giving back out, bringing the creation around you into your being and giving yourself back out into the world...

Allow yourself a sense of feeling part of everything created...

When you are ready to return, gradually lengthen your breathing, finally taking three long breaths to end your sitting.

12 ...to release the tension

Stress can come at all stages of our life.

It can be related to family, to work, to relationships, to illness...

It can be associated with going out, with staying in, with too much to do, with too little to do, with what we want, with what we don't want...

It feels like not coping, and not seeing a way to cope...

because there is always tension, between what is coming from outside us and what is available to meet it from inside.

This meditation speaks to those three aspects of stress - what is outside us that we feel as pressure, what is inside us and is holding on (but only just), and the tension we experience at the meeting point of the two.

Prepare yourself by sitting comfortably: check and physically loosen the muscles which you find are most apt to tense up for you...

... think-relax ...

Take three long breaths, as slowly and steadily as is comfortable...

... think-relax ...

As your breathing is slowly subsiding and your breaths are becoming shorter, see the in and out of your breathing as like a clock pendulum which swings slowly...

As the pendulum reaches the end of each swing it slows as it nears the turning point and pauses momentarily as it turns...

So... as each breath reaches its turning point, slow and pause for just a moment...

Maintain this as your breathing pattern and notice how it gives a **sense of rounding** *to your breathing, while you keep your drawing of breath at the same regular pace...*

Let this be your clear space; which rests you by dispersing your pressure and recuperates you with its peaceful turning.

When thoughts appear, hear them as if they were voices a little way away, far enough so that you cannot hear the words distinctly; as they go on talking let them move further and further away until, in the end, you can no longer hear them...

When you find yourself in your clear space with your

breathing, start to hear your own voice, softly perhaps but with firmness, repeating slowly this mantra:

being now being here is enough

Hear your voice with these words spreading throughout your body until all of you is resonating the chant, like a wave passing through you, no longer needing words...

Go back around this loop with the thoughts and your voice as many times as you need to...

When you are ready to end your sitting, slowly lengthen your breathing as you come out of meditation.

Themed Meditations ...along the quiet path

13 ...letting be

There is only so much we can do to convince another - we cannot *make* them change; there is only so much we can do to stop an argument - we can't *enforce* our view; there is only so much we can do to improve our neighbour's life - we must not disempower.

Just so much and then... we have to simply let it be as it will be.

However frustrated, however useless, however powerless we feel, we must simply stop and leave it.

To do otherwise would be to imply that we are better placed to decide what is best, what is right, when in reality 'best' and 'right' are relative to where we stand, in physical space, yes, but also in time.

Human kind have done their best to corrupt the planet, but in the end nature will win, because nature absorbs and assimilates. And we each are simply one of human kind.

This meditation is to help to find release through allowing that our resource is finite and that letting be without sorrow or reproach can be a kindness.

Check that you are sitting comfortably: check and physically loosen the muscles which you find are most apt to tense up for you...

Start to notice your breathing and let your attention rest on the even flow of your breath...

Gradually lengthen your breaths until you are breathing as deeply as is comfortable for you and then let your breathing subside again...

As your breaths shorten you can sense a slow descent like coming down a gentle slope towards an expanse of flat open space below...

As you sit at ease in your clear space, bring into your mind someone you know, in the sense of their being in their clear space, as you are in yours, each aware of each other but not limiting the other...

Now bring to mind another person you know and then **another and another** *in the same way...*

Now these several individuals can be around you, each in their own clear space, sometimes closer in your awareness, sometimes further away...

Bring each one in turn closer to you, each of you perhaps **speaking and listening**, *interacting a little and then moving away...*

When you are ready to end your meditation, be aware again of your own clear space for a few moments, then lengthen your breathing as you bring yourself back to the world around you.

14 ...to walk in harmony

This meditation is for outside. In principle it can be anywhere outside, though if you are not experienced at meditating, it would be better for it to be in as peaceful a location as possible. It should be somewhere that allows you to walk, not fast but not just sauntering either, without having to pay particular attention to avoiding collisions. It should also be fairly level so that breathing strain does not intrude.

To begin the meditation shake your body loose and just start walking in a comfortable way. Spend the first two or three minutes turning your attention to each group of muscles conveying the sense of *think-relax* to each. Spend a little more time on the muscles most affected by the action of walking, your hips and below.

Now start to notice how your steps fit in with your breathing. There is no need to *make* this rate of steps to breathing anything particular, but try to keep to a whole number for each breath and when you are comfortable look to maintain your walking at a constant rate.

Let your awareness be of the harmonious relation between your body, your breathing, your walking and the movement of your physical presence across the ground.

When you are feeling your **walking like a harmony** in this way, let your awareness widen to the space in which you are moving, so that this becomes part of your walking.

When the harmony includes the space too, let your attention widen still further to whatever is around you, the sky, the scenery, the people, and the way all of these complement your walking with the sense of space they create for you. They are also part of the harmony.

When you want to end your meditation, come to a halt and stand with your weight evenly distributed for a few moments, or sit with your feet in contact with the ground and your back straight.

Simon Cole

15 ...*on the experience of peace*

Peace is different from stillness; it is different even from silence, though both may be accompaniments.

Peace is a kind of non-interventionist fairy god-mother of our being, always just out of sight (because we don't look), but always available if we know how to summon her up, and always on our side. And just occasionally she appears of her own accord.

Peace is an absolute, it brooks no compromise and for each of us can only be an experience from within.

Here is a meditation to cultivate the experience of peace.

From a therapeutic perspective this meditation is about allowing our story to reconstruct and become the narrative which explains the person who is here now. Peace for each of us can only be the peace of the present and this can only come with the acknowledgement of our complete person, our whole story.

It is more important than ever, therefore, not to judge anything that appears as we allow ourselves that sense of how we are in the moment, aware that this person contains all the experiences of their life lived to this point. Not judging means not attaching 'good' or 'bad' labels to anything, but simply allowing everything to have been how it was.

You may find it helpful in this meditation to use the "breathing which strokes" (from the meditation "...to feel at ease") and to be particularly conscious of the out-breaths (the stroking breaths) each time you return to the feeling of being grounded.

Start with three long breaths and allow your out-breaths to smoothe the tensions in your muscles so that you can feel your whole body ease and relax...

Let your breathing subside into a gentle even rhythm...

Feel yourself moving into your clear space...

Feel the weight of your being, held by the earth, and be aware of this connection...

Let the earth take the weight *of your whole being, how it is now and how it has come to this point, and feel the comfort of that support...*

Allow yourself a sense of how you are, in this moment, at this point, which is the end-point so far of the path you have travelled and all that has happened to you...

Move gently between this sense and your feeling of comfort from the earth supporting, grounding you...

Feel the calm of this gentle movement, between the sense of your being at this moment and the feeling of being grounded, and let it resonate in your breathing...

Feel more and more the quiet firmness of the earth's support...

When you are ready, after your usual time of sitting, lengthen your breathing into three long breaths to bring yourself back.

16 ...of benevolence for our world

It is a natural extension of our meditation theme of being alive as a part of the community of all things living, that we should wish well (benevolence) for all people and everything living. If it falls to us to be able to actively help alleviate the difficulties of others (beneficence), then we are more fortunate still. But the process of simply wishing well, in the context of a meditation of benevolence, can also have a practical outcome, because in wishing well for others, we acknowledge their humanity.

If we can do this for people we do not know and cannot see, how much more is possible for those with whom we are in contact. Then we can see our own humanity, not as the centre of our individual world, but as a part of a world we are sharing.

Here is a meditation on this theme.

Start with three long breaths and allow your out-breaths to smoothe the tensions in your muscles so that you can feel your whole body ease and relax...

Let your breathing subside into a gentle even rhythm...

Feel yourself moving into your clear space...

Centre your attention on your body and how it feels to be supported by the earth below you, allowing you to feel your presence as a being in the world...

Let this become your felt sense of yourself at this moment and name the comfortable feelings that start to arise in you...

As you name each comfortable feeling, maybe one, maybe many, bring a person to mind that you would like to be feeling this same thing at this moment...

Continue to go round and round each feeling in turn, each time naming a new person that you would like to be feeling it...

As you continue to cycle round the feelings, individual names can become less important so that you extend your **benevolence** *to a wider and wider circle of people and then whole groups of people beyond your acquaintance...*

When you are ready, after your usual time of sitting, lengthen your breathing into three long breaths to bring yourself back.

Simon Cole

ABOUT THE AUTHOR

Simon Cole BA(Econ) MA(Counselling) MBACP(Snr Acc) has been a practising counsellor and therapist for 30 years. After working for several years with the Samaritans, he qualified as a counsellor at Newcastle University and gained a Masters degree with distinction from Ripon & York St John (then affiliated to Leeds University), later training with Joseph Zinker during his UK visits. Author of articles for counselling journals in the UK and Australia, he worked for many years within NHS primary and secondary care, whilst leading the counsellor training programmes at diploma level at Carlisle College. For the last seven years he has run a residential retreat centre in southwest France with his wife. The emphasis is on a therapy which picks up the natural rhythm of the surroundings and works with self- discovery through mindfulness and meditation, combined with creative counselling, music, poetry and writing. Mindfulness and meditation have for many years been a vital part of his life and have formed an increasingly significant part of his therapeutic approach with the formalising of the Clear Space Meditation Path.

web: www.life-counselling.co.uk email: simoncole.france@gmail.com

Simon Cole

Made in the USA
Charleston, SC
31 January 2015